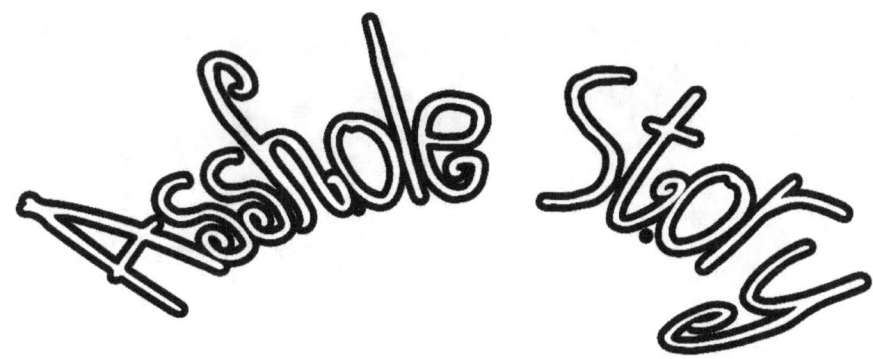

Asshole Story

Adorable Swear Word To Color

FOR STRESS RELEASING

By

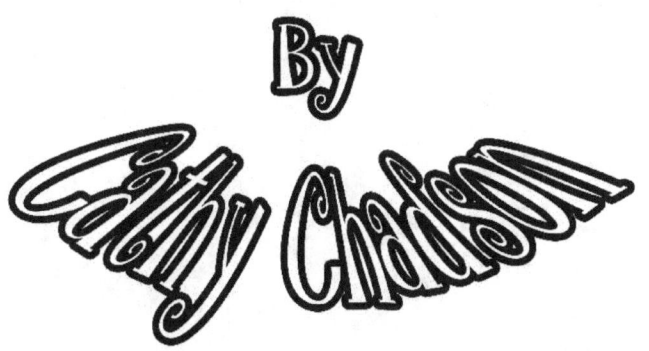

Happy Coloring

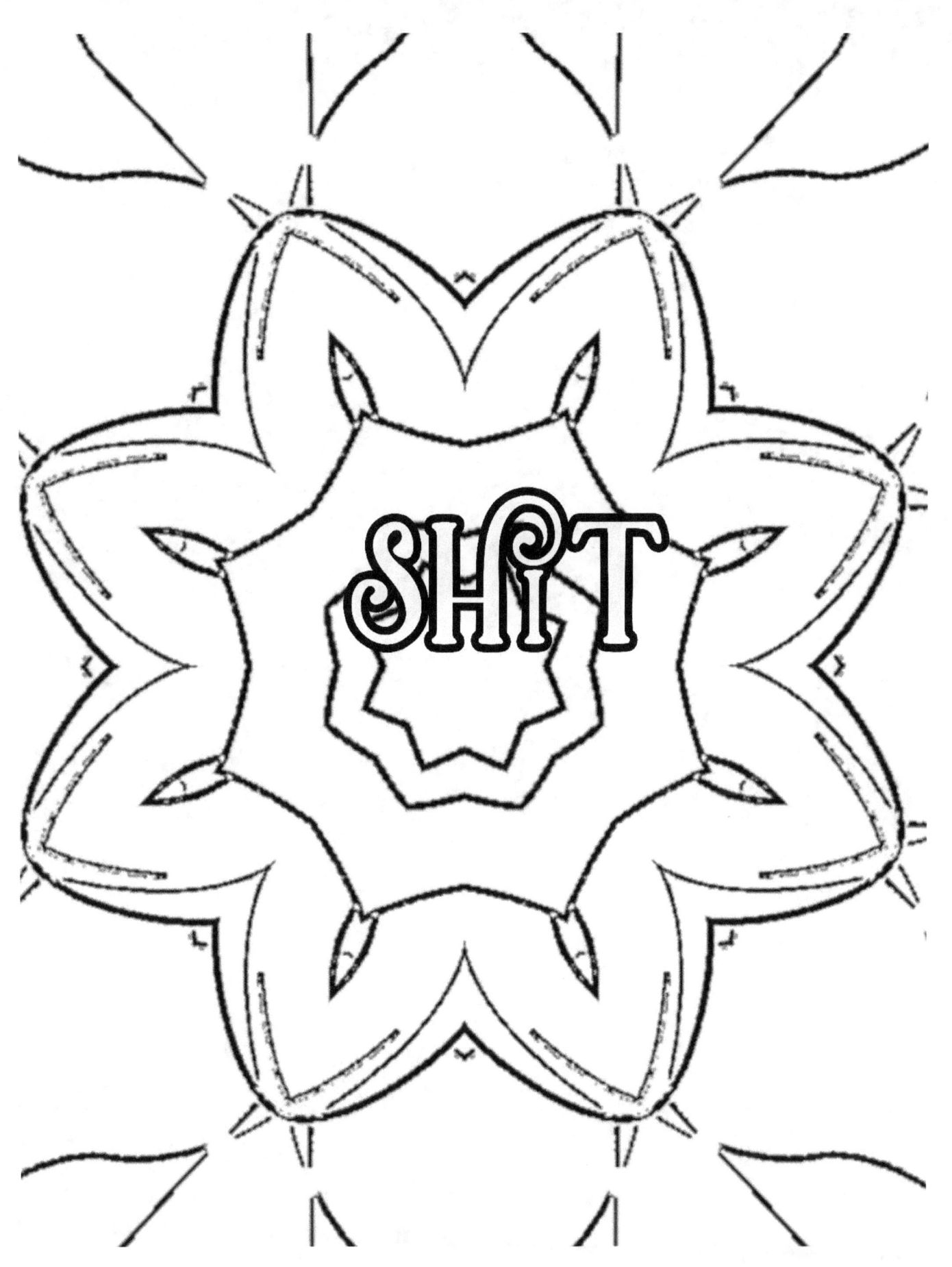

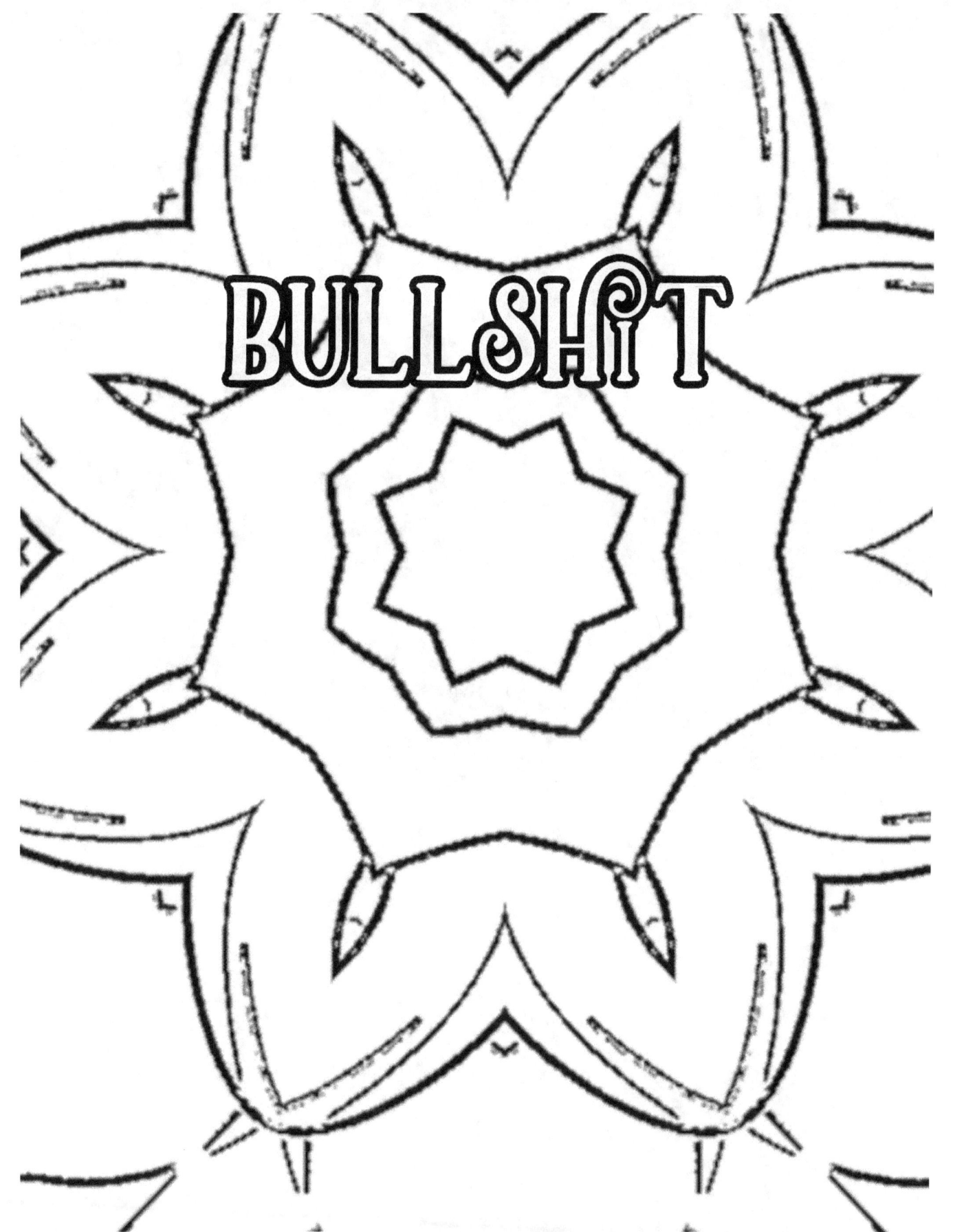

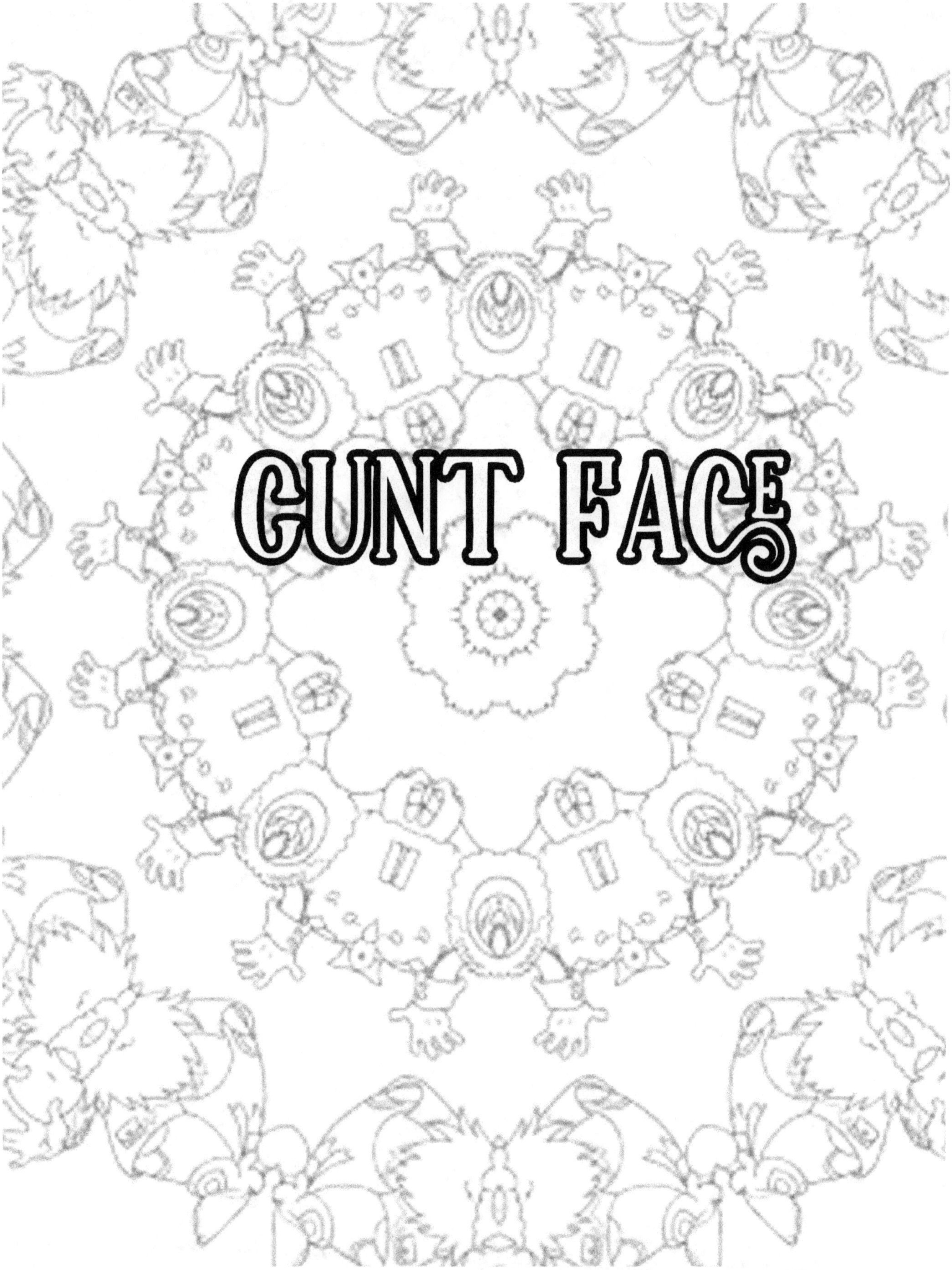
CUNT FACE

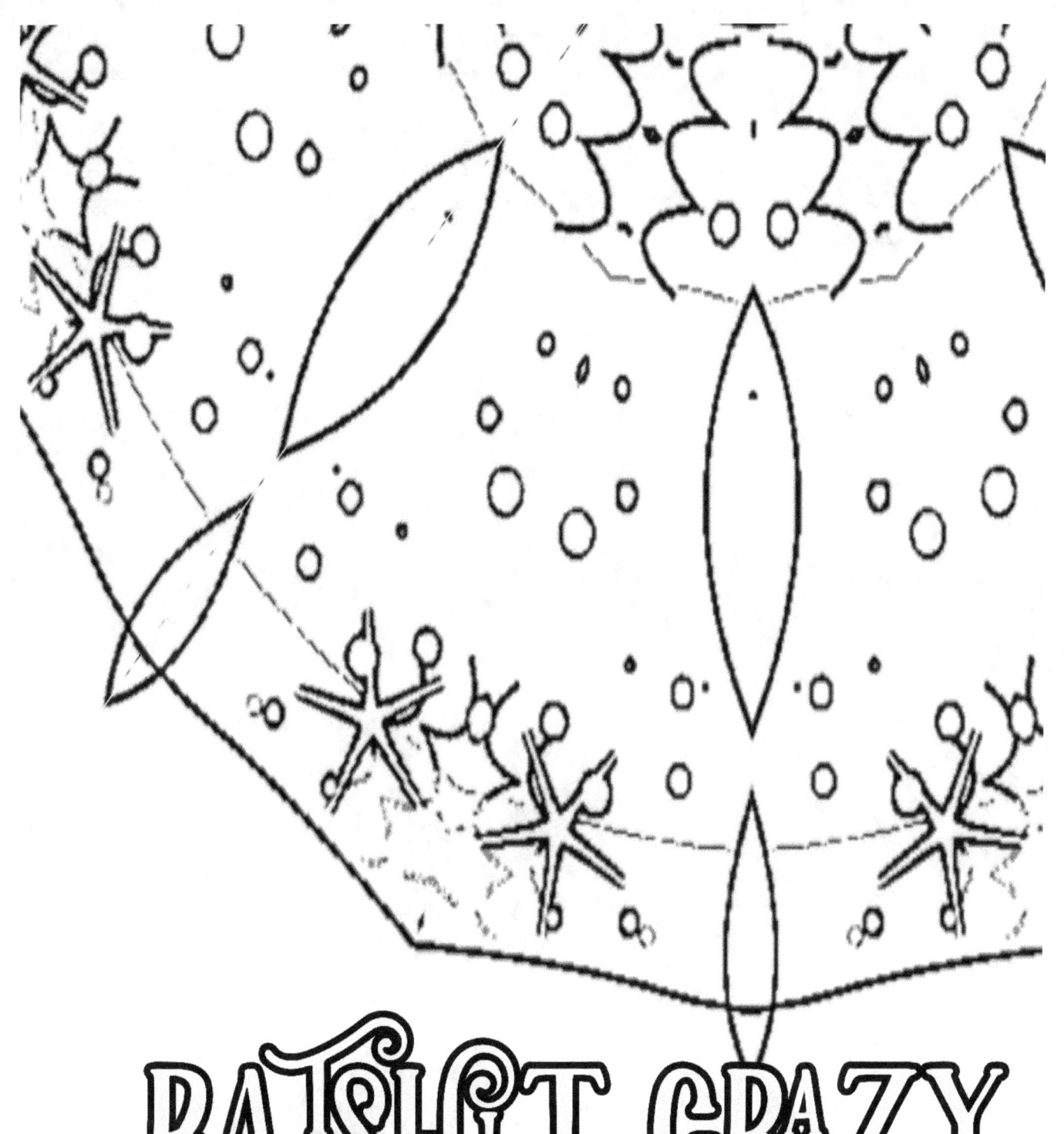

BATSHIT CRAZY

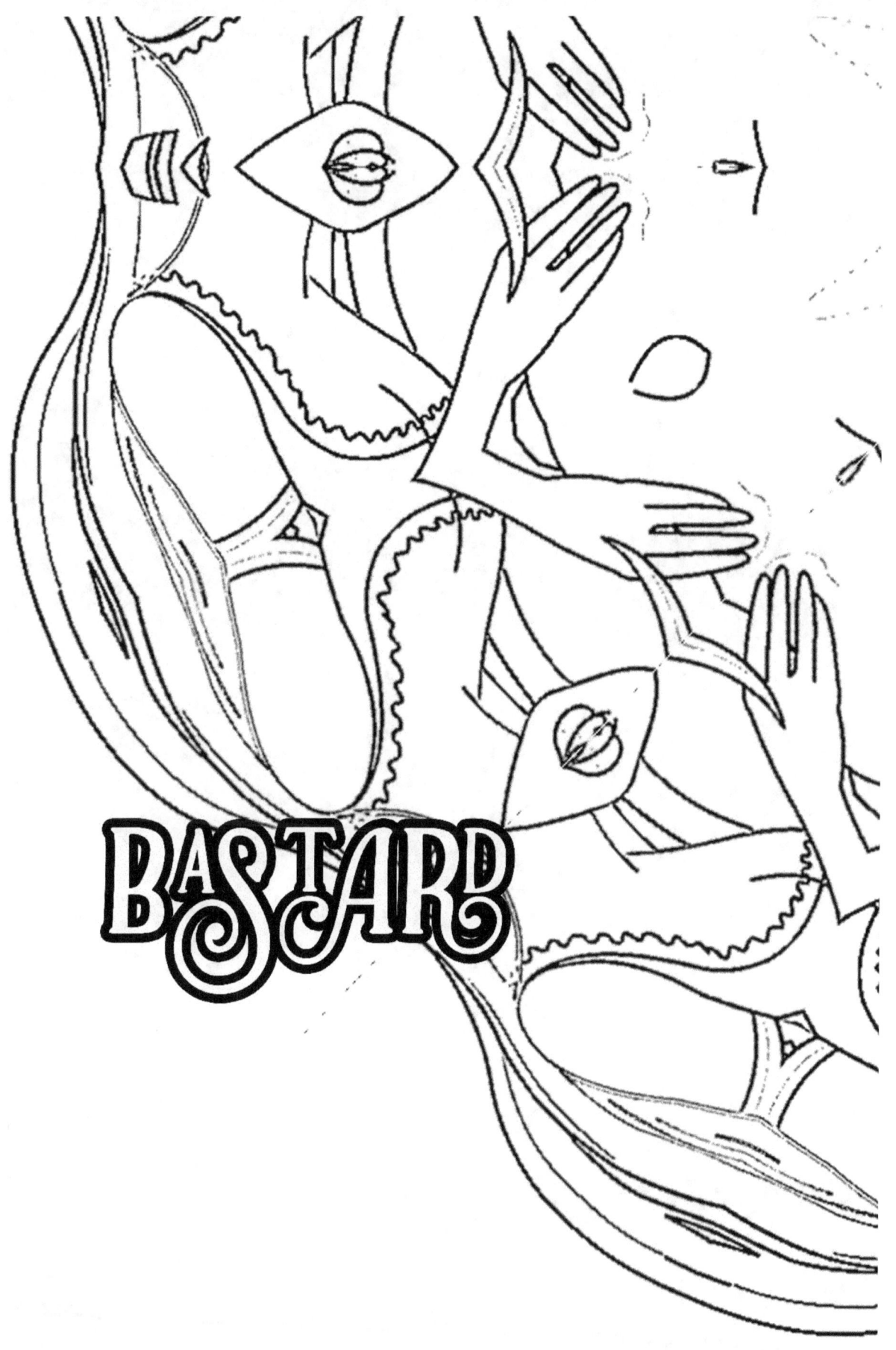

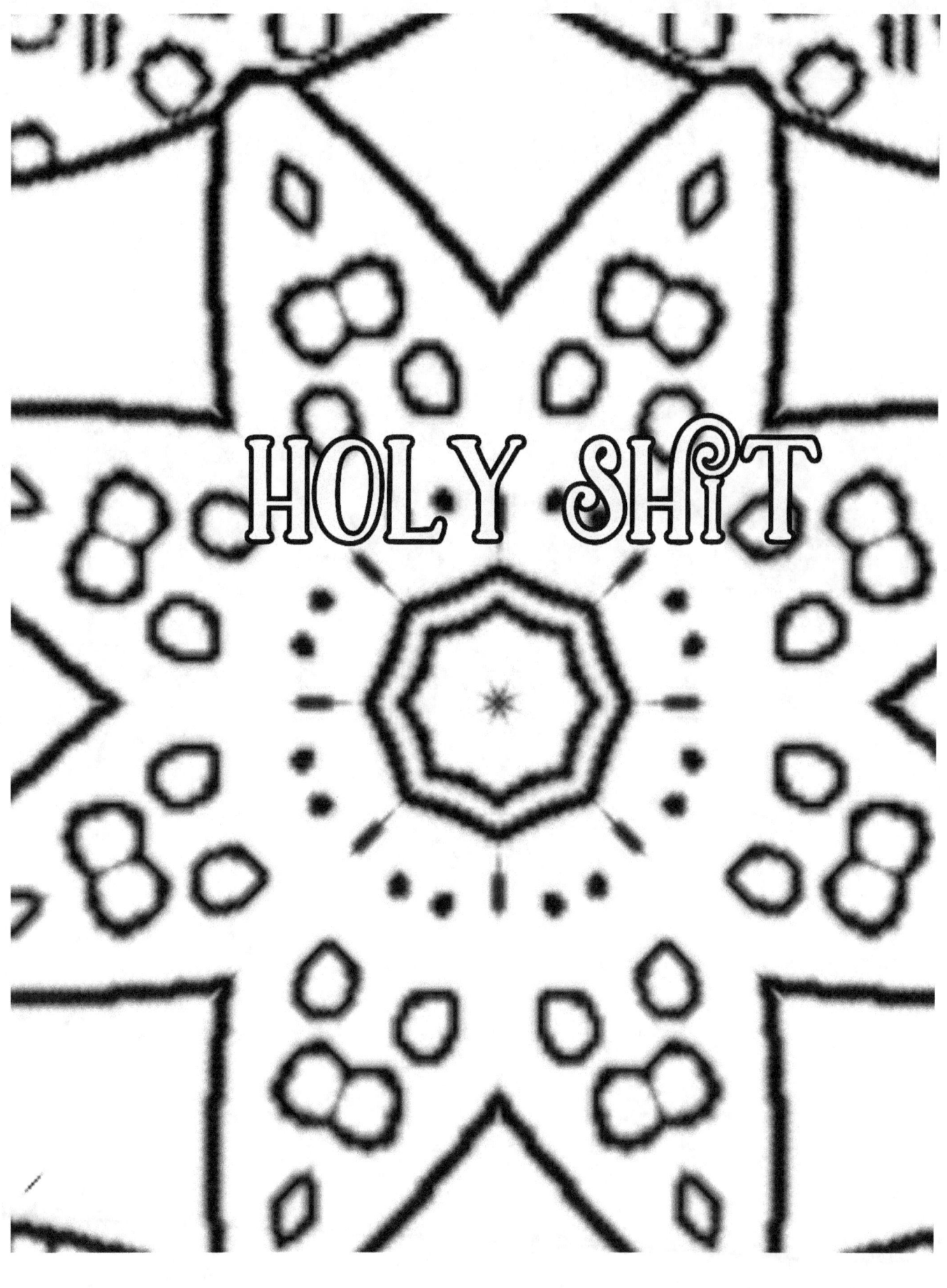

ASSHOLE

DOUCHE BAG

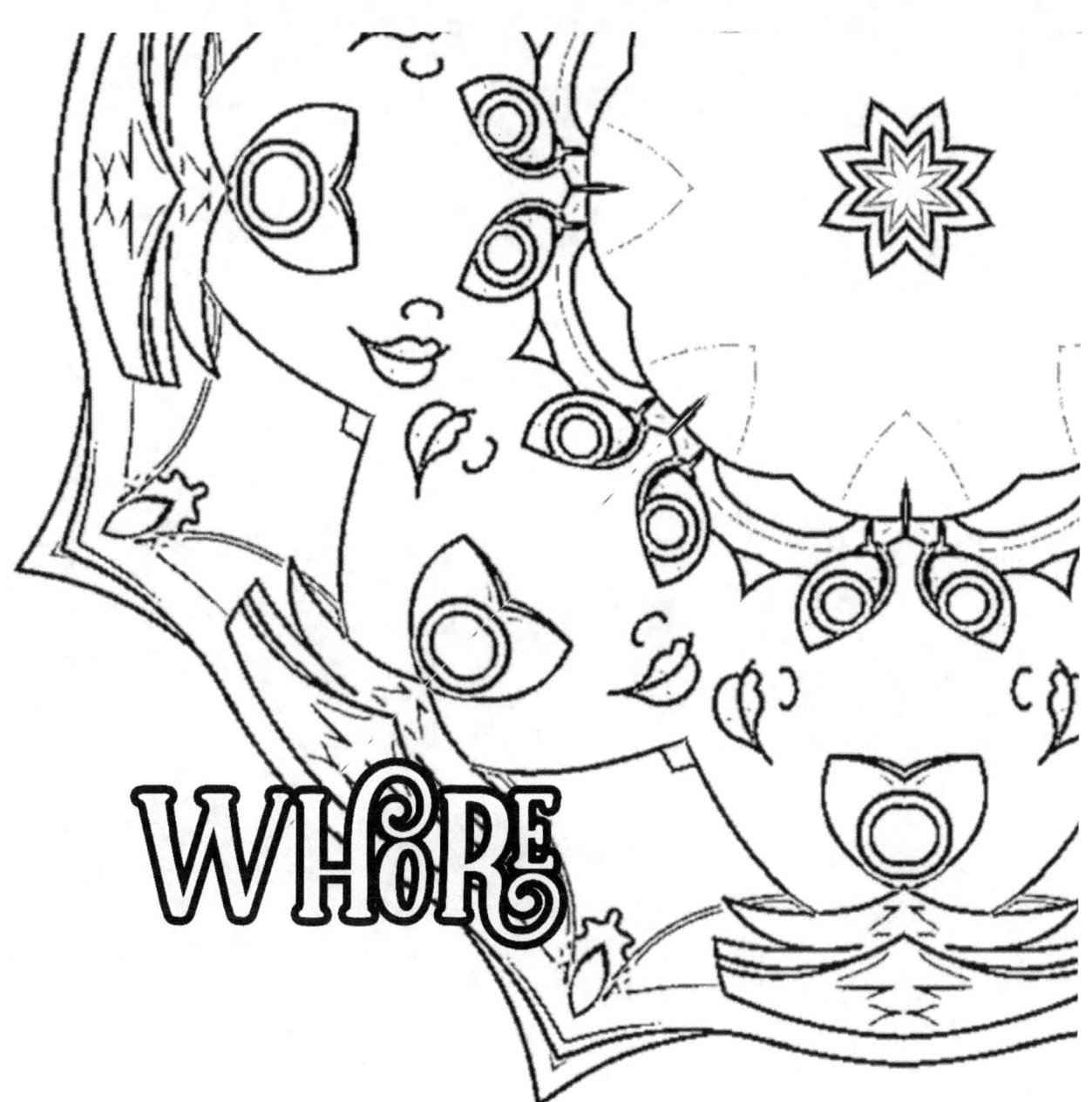

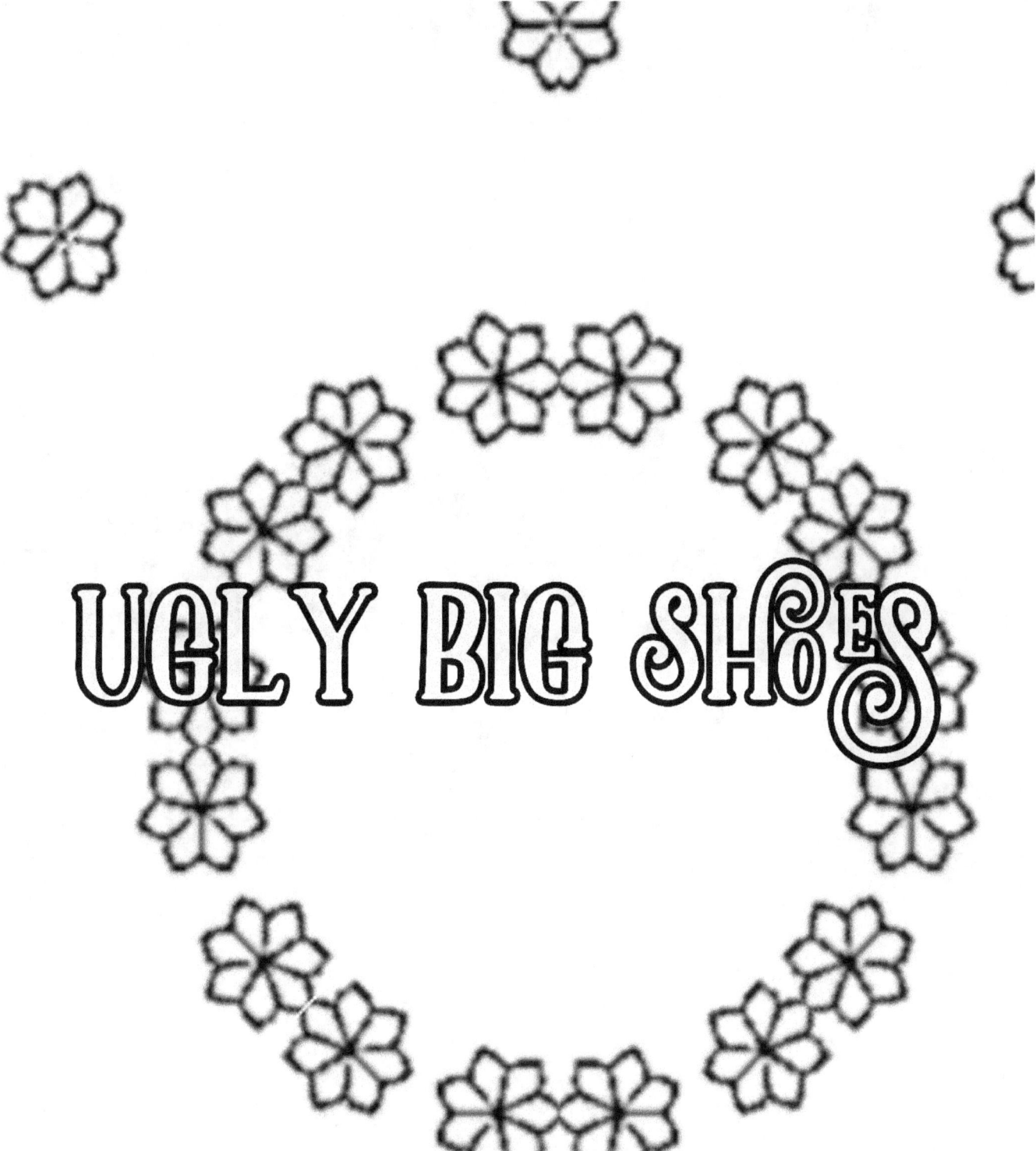

UGLY BIG SHOES

DICK MIDGET

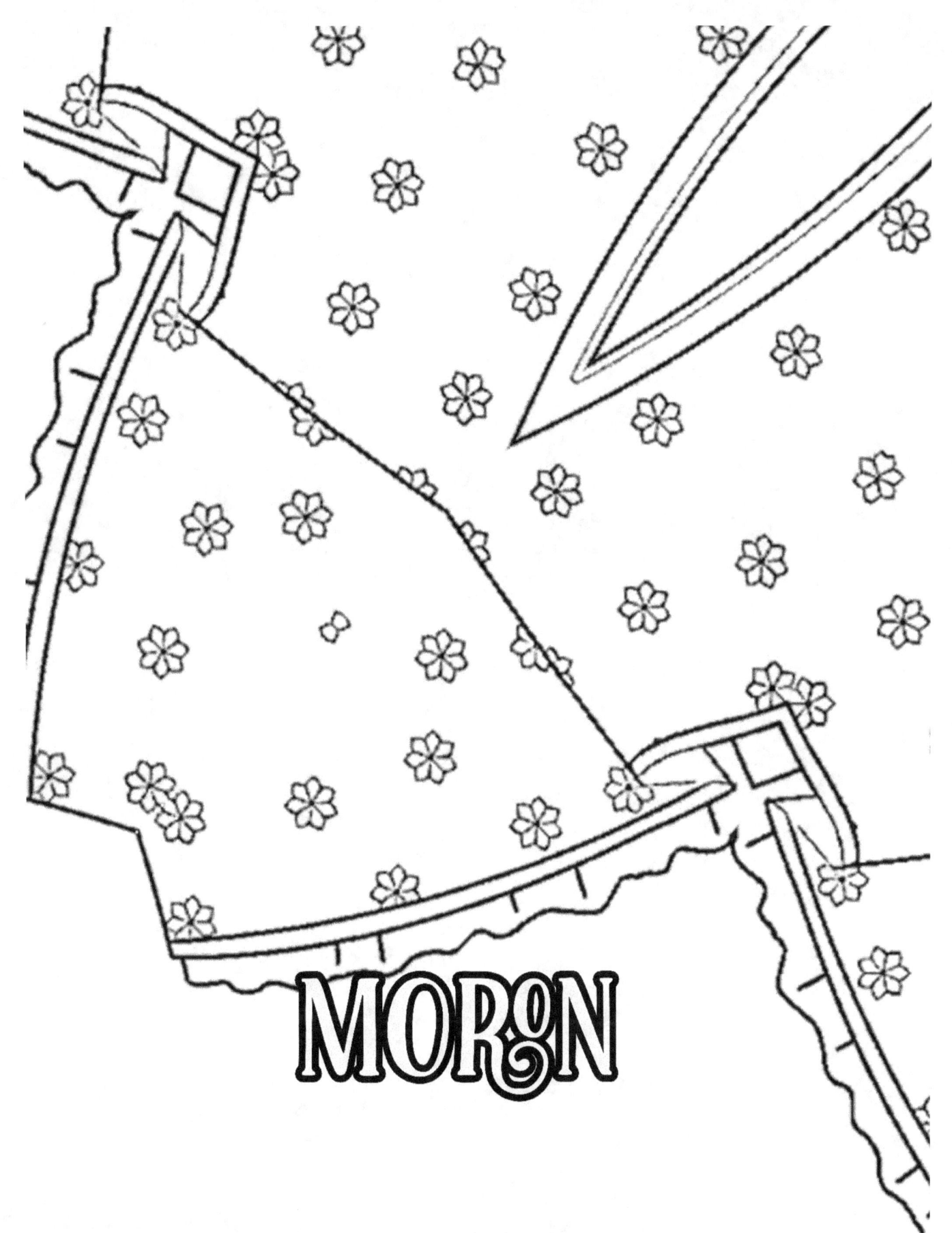

MORON

OLD FART

LOW LIFE

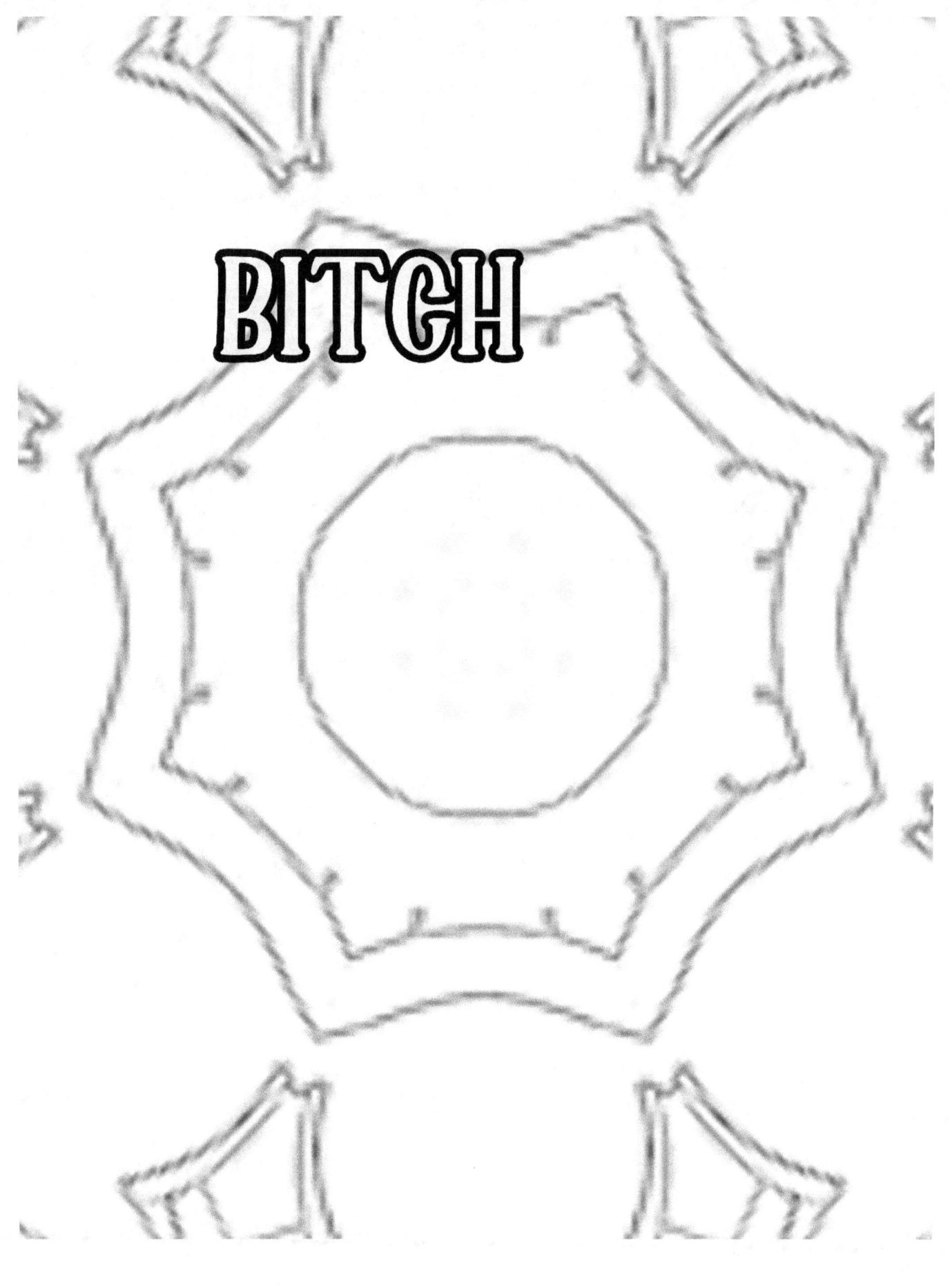

PISS OFF

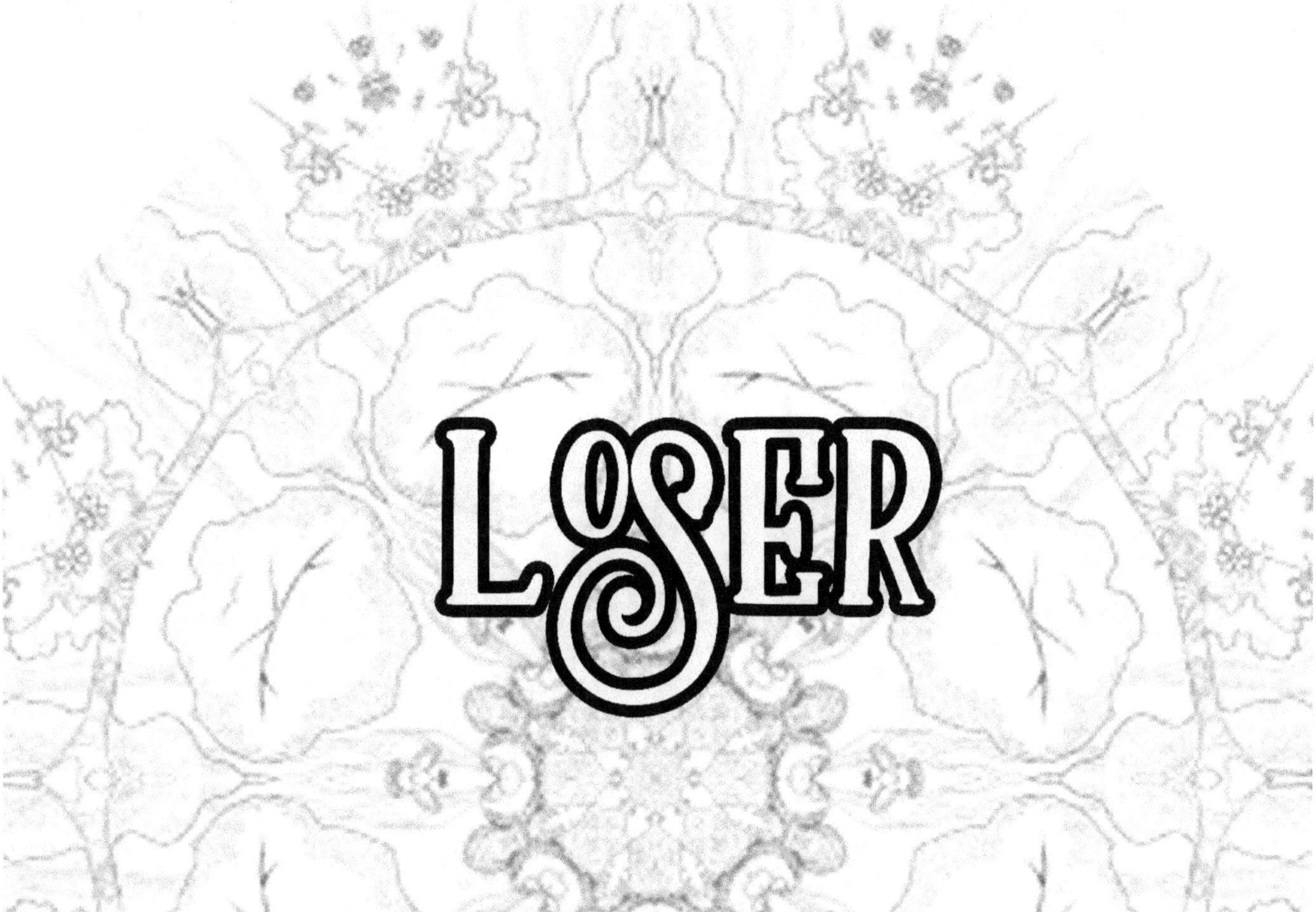
LOSER

DICKHEAD

FUCK A DUCK

ATTENTION WHORE

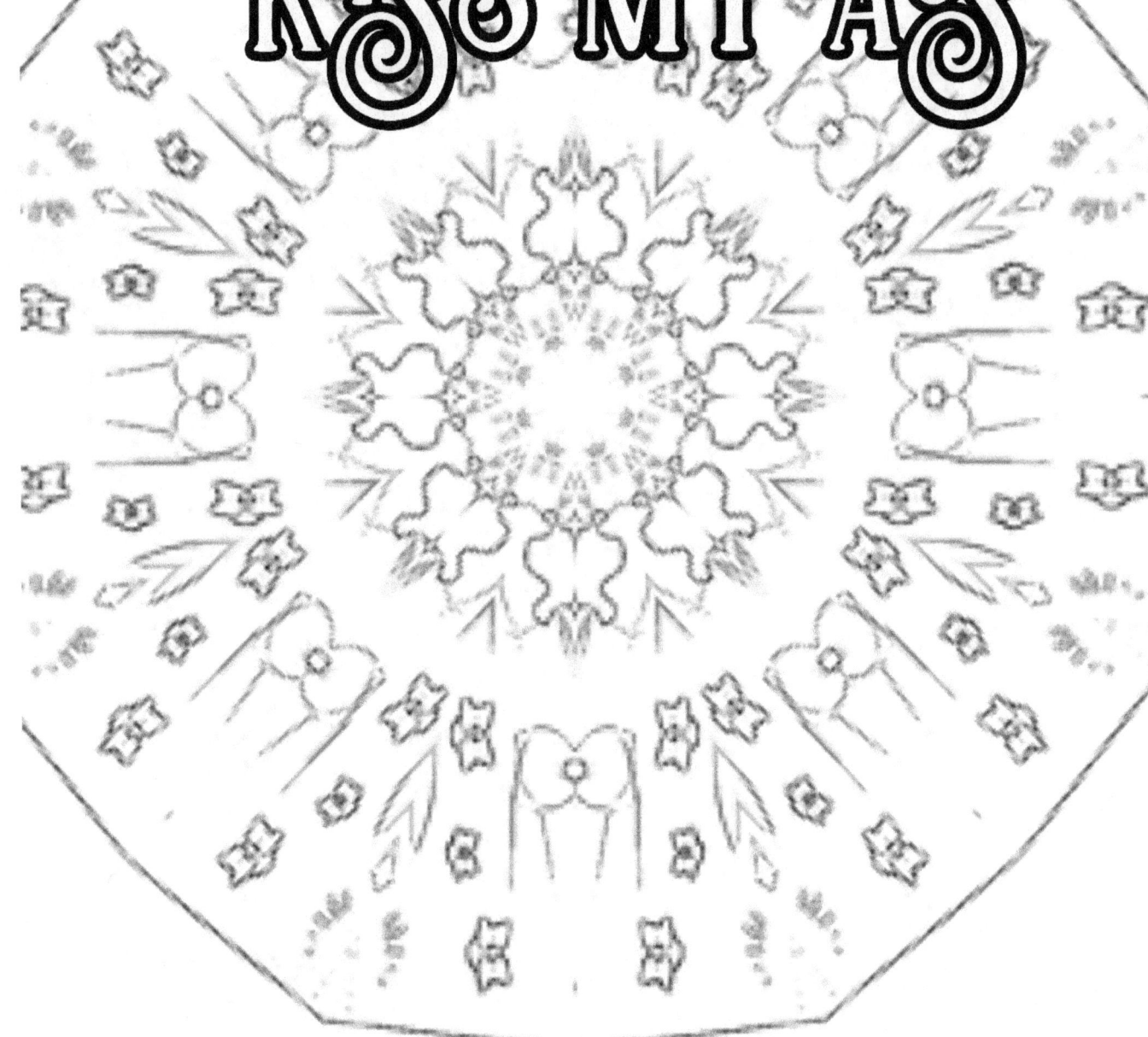

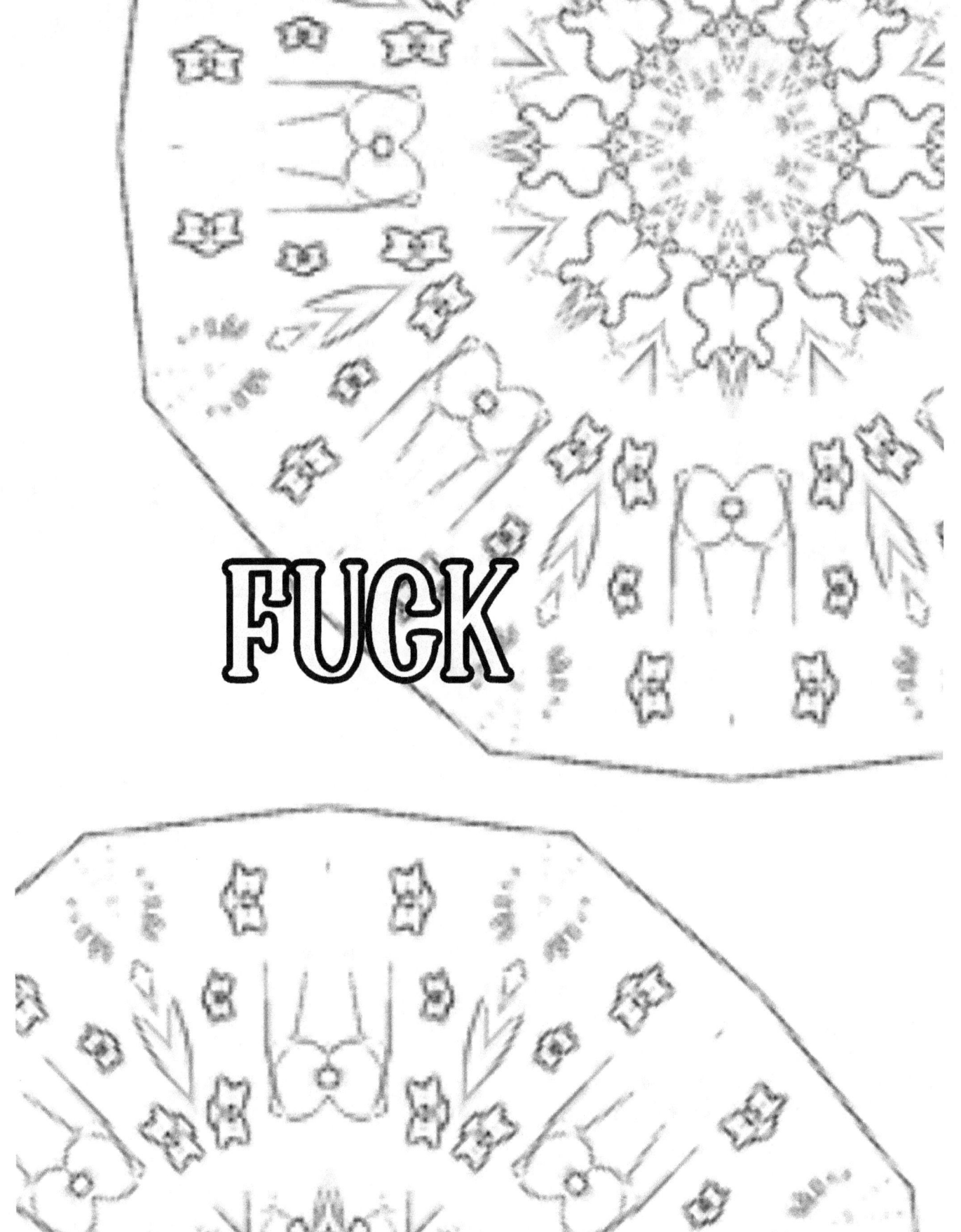

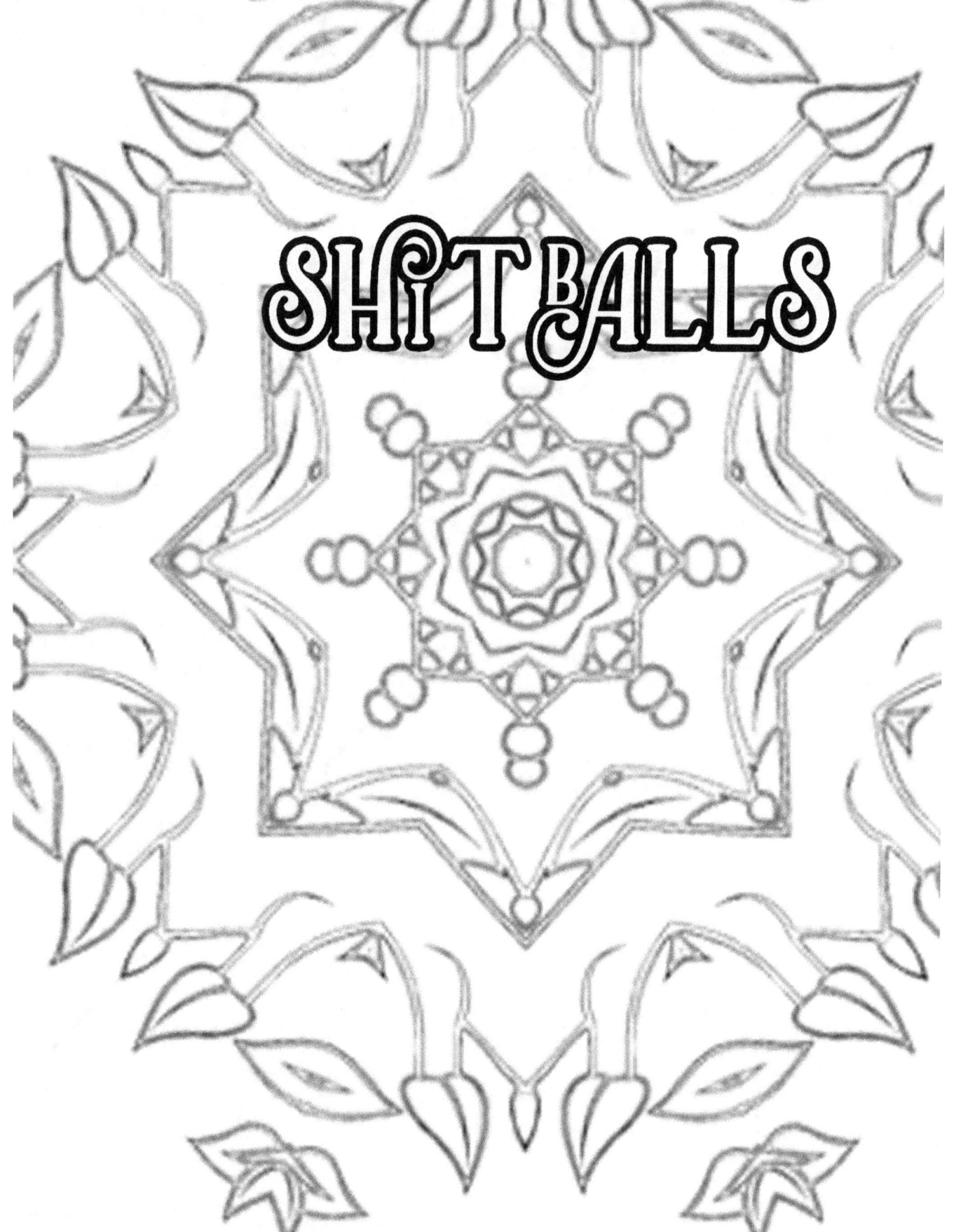

DIPSHITIDIOT

WHAT AN ASS

www.ingramcontent.com/pod-product-compliance
Lightning Source LLC
Chambersburg PA
CBHW081747170526
45167CB00009B/3954